DELTA**BLUES**
SLIDEGUITAR

A Complete Guide to Authentic Acoustic Blues Slide Guitar Technique

LEVI**CLAY**

FUNDAMENTAL**CHANGES**

Delta Blues Slide Guitar

An Introduction to Acoustic Blues Slide Guitar Technique

Published by www.fundamental-changes.com

ISBN 978-1-78933-014-4

www.fundamental-changes.com

Twitter: **@guitar_joseph**

Over 10,000 fans on Facebook: **FundamentalChangesInGuitar**

Instagram: **FundamentalChanges**

For over 350 Free Guitar Lessons with Videos Check Out

www.fundamental-changes.com

Cover image reproduced with the kind permission of Manny Ruiz

Contents

Introduction   4

Get the Audio   6

Chapter One – Slides and Guitar Setup   7

Chapter Two – Fretting With The Slide   11

Chapter Three – Sliding Between Notes   19

Chapter Four – Vibrato   24

Chapter Five – Open Tuning Scales   28

Chapter Six – One String Scales   35

Chapter Seven – Open Position Playing   46

Chapter Eight – Saint Louis Blues   55

Chapter Nine – Melodies And Bass   58

Chapter Ten – Changing Chords   69

Chapter Eleven – Fretting Notes Using Fingers   81

Chapter Twelve – Solo Blues   90

Chapter Thirteen – Blues Rag   98

Conclusion   105

Other Books by Levi Clay   107

Introduction

The history and development of slide, or *bottleneck* guitar can be traced back over 100 years across multiple continents. The basic idea can be seen in the "diddley bow" in early colonized America. West African slaves would stretch a single string across a wooden board and use a glass bottle as a bridge. A piece of metal would then be pressed against the string to change its pitch.

Similarly, as the Spanish guitar made its way to Hawaii, the natives began to detune the strings to an open chord (commonly referred to as *slack-key* guitar), then play the guitar on their laps, using a steel bar to fret the strings. This Hawaiian *steel guitar* sound quickly spread, with innovators like Joseph Kekuku becoming a big hit in early 1900s American vaudeville shows.

As time went on, performers in the Mississippi Delta began using other hard objects – such as knives, medicine bottles, copper pipes and the necks of glass bottles (bottlenecks!) – as tools to create a more expressive sound with their instrument. Using a slide, they were able to more closely imitate the way the human voice can smoothly slide from one pitch to another, and capture all the microtones found between the well-established twelve tone pitch system of the West.

The first recordings of this style were played by Sylvester Weaver in 1923. His *Guitar Rag* and *Guitar Blues* would heavily influence the evolving blues scene in the Mississippi Delta, along with the music of many travelling musicians who weren't fortunate enough to be recorded. From this scene would emerge iconic names such as Robert Johnson, Son House and Bukka White – all of whom are well respected by fans and historians alike.

Over time, the blues scene began to take a backseat to rock, jazz, and other styles that became popular in the dance halls. It wasn't until young musicians in the UK began to get their hands on imported records from the Delta that a new explosion of blues took the world by storm. While the big names of British blues like Peter Green, Eric Clapton, Jeff Beck, Jimmy Page etc, aren't best known for playing slide, it's certainly something they were influenced by and picked up from time to time.

This book will focus on the Delta blues style before the rise of amplification and electric guitar soloing, but it's worth pointing out that slide guitar has never died out. While there are still some incredible musicians around like Keb' Mo', keeping the original Delta spirit alive, slide guitar has been taken to extraordinary heights by the likes of Ry Cooder, Derek Trucks, Sonny Landreth and Bonnie Raitt. Slide guitar has also appeared on legendary recordings by the likes of Led Zeppelin, Derek and the Dominos, The Allman Brothers Band and The Beatles

It's no secret that blues purists are very specific about their area of expertise, so it's important to clarify that this book will focus on the Delta blues roots. From this style evolved the various American blues subgenres that include Chicago blues, Country blues, Texas blues, Jump blues and more, up to the British blues revival of the 1950s.

What this means is that this book focuses on playing the Delta music as authentically as possible. You won't find many twelve-bar blues progressions here. It's not a lick book and it's important you understand the essence of the Delta sound before jumping in. Early Delta music was normally played by a single musician using riff-based, repetitive figures on the guitar to accompany their voice. Any licks were simply fills between the rhythm guitar parts that were, again, repetitive and largely functional.

Before you get started, check out the artists listed below and make sure you're familiar with their music and style.

If you're expecting a book on twelve-bar slide guitar playing in the style of Duane Allman or Derek Trucks, in the words of Lemony Snicket, look away now! This book is a journey to the first vestiges of the blues that began to appear almost 60 years before Led Zeppelin and Eric Clapton brought blues to the masses, and decades before it was first recorded in 1920.

One final thing to remember: this style was popularised by the music of impoverished African Americans who sang about the unbelievable hardships they and their parents had faced, and were still enduring. I'm not saying you need to have a real understanding of slavery to "get" the blues, but it's worth remembering that the people playing this music were not academics. They had very little, if any, education and even less when it came to music. That said, to teach anything we need to break it down into individual concepts and ideas and some of the material in this book will need to be analysed in terms of "Western" music theory, simply so I can explain what's going on and how to recreate it.

Theory is something that's written down *after* the music has been made so we can explain it to others. It's simply one way of talking about sound. I use simple music theory in this book to communicate with you about how to recreate Delta music on your guitar and it's not my intention to turn to roots of the blues into a rigid, academic subject. Once I've described what's going on in the music, please try to get the *sound* and *feeling* of the examples into your head and forget as much of the academic stuff as possible. It's so important to download the audio examples.

This style isn't about learning and applying theory, and can never be processed in a cold, clinical manner. It's all about attitude and playing from the heart. So don't overthink it, just play!

Levi

Recommended listening:

- Sylvester Weaver – Complete Recorded Works in Chronological Order Volume 1

- Robert Johnson – The Complete Recordings

- Son House – Son House Library of Congress Recordings 1941 – 1942

- Bukka White – High Fever Blues: The Complete 1930 – 1940 Recordings

- Blind Willie Johnson – The Spiritual Blues

- Blind Willie McTell – King Of The Serpent Blues

- Tampa Red – You Can't Get That Stuff No More

- Charley Patton – The Definitive Charley Patton

- Blind Boy Fuller – Get Your Yas Yas Out

- Leadbelly – The Very Best of Leadbelly

- Elmore James – The Sky Is Crying

- Muddy Waters – The Chess Singles Collection

- Lightnin' Hopkins – Dirty House Blues

Get the Audio

The audio files for this book are available to download for free from **www.fundamental-changes.com.** The link is in the top right-hand corner. Simply select this book title from the drop-down menu and follow the instructions to get the audio.

We recommend that you download the files directly to your computer, not to your tablet, and extract them there before adding them to your media library. You can then put them on your tablet, iPod or burn them to CD. On the download page there is a help PDF and we also provide technical support via the contact form.

For over 350 Free Guitar Lessons with Videos Check out:

www.fundamental-changes.com

Twitter: **@guitar_joseph**

Over 10,000 fans on Facebook: **FundamentalChangesInGuitar**

Instagram: **FundamentalChanges**

Chapter One – Slides and Guitar Setup

I'm sure you're eager to get to the music, but it's important to begin with some equipment and technical discussion. In the first four chapters we will discuss the best setup for slide guitar, how to play a note in tune with the correct *intonation*, how to move between notes, and finally one of the most crucial playing techniques: *vibrato*. Vibrato is an essential tool for any type of slide guitar playing and it's one of the most defining factors in creating an authentic, pleasing sound.

Slide choice

There is endless debate about what material works best for a guitar slide. Ultimately, it should be about what gives you the sound you desire.

The two most common materials are glass and metal. I have a collection of slides made from many materials, including glass, ceramic, brass and steel. They all have a different sound and I use them for different things. Personally, I find I like heavier, thicker slides, so I'm fond of brass or glass. Brass slides tend to have more treble in their tone and, because they are rarely as smooth as glass, are a bit noisier – which is ideal for a rootsy Delta sound.

Most of the recordings that accompany this book were recorded using a Dunlop 222 Medium Brass slide. It's nothing fancy, but it gets the job done. If you want something a little bit more boutique, The Rock Slide (www.therockslide.com) offer a great selection of slides made from different materials and with features such as tapered interiors and finger rests. They also come personally recommended!

Guitar setup

When it comes to slide playing, the main factor in making it as easy as possible is your guitar setup. The essence of slide technique is pressing the slide against the strings so that it acts like a fret. We want to avoid a situation where the pressure of the slide pressing against the string causes it to make contact with the fretboard. A higher action will make playing slide guitar much easier.

"Action" refers to the height of your strings from the fretboard. A lower action results in less effort being required to fret a note, but the compromise is that minor inconsistencies in fret height can result in spots where the strings buzz against the frets when plucked. A higher action means that the guitar requires us to work a bit harder to play it, but generally results in a purer tone from the instrument.

On most electric guitars, there are ways to raise the action at the bridge, but this has most impact higher up the neck and less impact at the nut. For an ideal setup, you might consider having a new nut fitted that's a little taller than the factory setup. This isn't essential (I've personally never changed the nut on my electric guitars), but it can help if you're struggling to get used to the lightness of touch required for this technique.

Acoustic or resonator guitars generally come out of the factory with a higher setup than electric guitars, so if you're using one, you will most likely be OK. Don't forget, however, that as your playing develops, fine-tuning your guitar setup can help to enhance your playing style.

Most players will use the slide in conjunction with fretted notes, so your action shouldn't be so high that fretting notes lower down becomes a Herculean task. If, on the other hand, you plan to use the slide only, there are some great products available such as the Grover Perfect Nut. This is a metal nut cover that sits over the top of your existing nut to raise the action of your strings to lap steel height.

Plucking the strings

Then there is the question of how you will use your picking hand. It is possible to use a pick, but using the thumb and fingers enables us to have much more control over techniques such as muting strings and controlling the tone being produced. When playing fingerstyle, it's possible to use the flesh of the fingers, or a combination of thumb pick and finger picks. Again, it all comes down to sound and feel. Using any sort of pick will give you a brighter attack on each note which may, or may not, be more desirable for your personal goals. As always, experiment and don't be afraid to stick to what works for you.

For reference, I recorded most of the audio for this book using a Tanglewood TMR Tricone resonator guitar. The heavy steel body results in a wonderfully unique tone that's hard to achieve on a traditional steel string guitar. The guitar was strung with D'Addario .013 – .056 gauge 80/20 Bronze strings, and was recorded with Shure SM57 and SM7b microphones.

Wearing the slide

While it's possible to adapt any of the ideas in this book to use a steel bar, it's assumed that 99% of readers will be playing with a slide designed to be placed on a finger. The first dilemma any aspiring slide player faces then, is which finger to place it on! For reasons that will become apparent when we get into the exercises, the index finger is not a good choice. That leaves the middle, ring and pinky fingers. I could name notable players as evidence of the superiority of each finger, but the truth is, there is no clear winner. Each option has its pros and cons and you'll quickly become comfortable with whichever you choose.

The sensible option is to try your slide on each finger and go with the one that feels most natural. I would suggest that, for the Delta blues style, the pinky is probably the wisest choice. It frees up three fingers to perform other tasks as needed.

I learned with the slide on my ring finger, then switched to my middle finger for many years. For the last 18 months or so I have tried to make my pinky finger the default. Nothing is set in stone and once you understand the technique required for slide, you should find adapting relatively simple.

Tuning

The final consideration for the aspiring slide guitar player is the tuning of the guitar itself. Playing slide guitar in standard tuning is perfectly possible, but a trickier prospect for the beginner, since you can't fret the slide and strum all six strings at once to make a pleasing sound. For this reason, early blues musicians opted for the classic *slack-key* open tunings, where the six strings are tuned to the notes of a chord. This way, when strummed, all of the notes are in key.

While it's possible to become proficient in many open tunings, it's more common for players to choose one to master. In this book we will focus mostly on open D, but we'll dabble in open G too. These are two of the most popular tunings amongst Delta blues musicians.

"Open D" tuning means that the strings are tuned to the notes of a D Major chord. D Major contains the notes D, F# and A. You can tune your guitar to open D as follows:

- Begin with standard tuning – E A D G B E

- Tune the low E string down a tone to D

- The A string stays the same (already in a D Major chord)

- The D string stays the same (already in a D Major chord)

- Tune the G string down a semitone to F#

- Tune the B string down a tone to A

- Tune the high E string down a tone to D

You're now tuned to open D tuning – D A D F# A D

It would be worth practising this by taking a guitar with standard tuning, tuning it to open D, then putting it back into standard tuning several times. This way you're getting an understanding of what the tuning name means and how to create it.

Here's an example of the six strings tuned to open D, played individually and then as a chord.

Example 1a:

Now that you understand how to tune to open D, open G should be fairly easy to achieve. A G Major chord contains the notes G, B and D.

- Begin with standard tuning – E A D G B E

- Tune the low E string down a tone to D

- Tune the A string down a tone to G

- The D string stays the same (already in a G Major chord)

- The G string stays the same (already in a G Major chord)

- The B string stays the same (already in a G Major chord)

- Tune the high E string down a tone to D

You're now tuned to open G tuning – D G D G B D.

Example 1b:

With that knowledge under your belt, it should be possible to tune your guitar to almost any chord by taking the notes of that chord and tuning your strings to the nearest pitch. For example, an E Major chord contains the notes E, G# and B, so open E tuning is E B E G# B E, and so on.

There are no rules for tunings, only what's common. When you hear someone say something like, "I tune to open C" this could mean different things to different people. Many players would assume it means C G C G C E, but I can think of players who tune to C G C E G C. Both are perfectly valid "open C" tunings.

Because of these possible tuning variations, I've opted to label everything in this book based on the string number rather than the note it's tuned to. This way there's no confusion when switching between tunings. Referring to the F# string in open D confuses me and I've been playing for a long time!

In this book, the highest tuned string is labelled the "first string", the next is the second string, then the third, and so on.

Chapter Two – Fretting With The Slide

This section teaches you great slide technique and how to produce clean, sustained notes. The lessons here will affect every single note you play, so work slowly through each example and try to match your sound to the downloadable audio tracks.

The first thing to understand is how to produce a note with the slide and make sure it's in tune. To do this, we must fully understand what the slide does and how it creates a pitch.

When I began playing slide, I assumed you used the slide to press the string down, as an alternative to the fretting finger. This couldn't be more misguided!

When fretting a note, we push the string down so that it comes into contact with the fret. The string will then vibrate from the fret to the bridge. The shorter this distance, the faster the string will vibrate and the higher the pitch it produces. When we fret a note with a finger, we can apply pressure anywhere between the adjacent fret wires and the string will touch the fret. But when we are using the slide, it must be placed exactly above the fret wire.

Using a slide is like controlling a moveable fret. The slide makes contact with the string and applies enough pressure so that the string vibrates between the slide and the bridge. I'll say it again: for a note to be in tune, the slide must be placed *exactly* over the fret.

In Example 2a I play the high D string open, then fret with the slide at the 12th fret – D an octave higher. To be in tune the slide must be positioned right where the string would touch the fret.

Example 2a:

Now listen to Example 2b. It's notated the same way, but on the audio I have positioned the slide halfway between the frets.

Example 2b:

Now I'll address how I fret this note with the slide and what my other fingers are doing. When playing with a slide it's possible that the strings can vibrate between the slide and the bridge, *and* the slide and the nut. These "sympathetic" vibrations can occasionally be used to great effect, but 99% of the time they're undesirable. Therefore, it's important to use the fingers behind the slide as a mute by resting them on the strings to stop any unwanted vibrations.

Here's an example chord played at the 12th fret. I'll play it twice without any muting, then twice muting the strings behind the slide.

Example 2c:

In this instance, the sympathetic vibrations are perfectly fine because the chord is played at the 12th fret – the halfway point of the neck – so the string will produce the same frequency in front and behind the string.

Now listen to this same exercise with a chord played at the 8th fret. The chord is lower, but the strings vibrating behind the slide are higher in pitch and clash with the notes we want the audience to hear. In this case muting is essential.

Example 2d:

Muting behind the slide is an essential technique. It's not a rule, and some players would throw it right out the window, but muting will give you a cleaner, more focused sound. Not muting will result in a more raw, rough around the edges sound. But playing music is about expressing yourself, and it's great to have all the tools at your disposal.

Now you understand how to play notes that are in tune, the next step is to play a series of notes.

Example 2e moves between the 12th and 10th frets. At this stage, we are primarily concerned with the pitch accuracy of the notes. Listen to the audio and pay attention to exactly what it sounds like. Play the first note twice, then move to the next note by lifting the slide off the string. When doing this, use the plucking hand to mute the string so that the transition is clean.

Example 2e:

Here's another example, this time playing the full D Minor Pentatonic scale (D F G A C) on the high D string. (Obviously, this isn't particularly representative of Delta blues playing, but exercises like this are extremely valuable as they force us to concentrate on achieving good intonation. They're a valuable use of your time, so don't skip them!)

Example 2f:

When playing an example like this I angle the slide so that it *only* makes contact with the high D string and avoids any extraneous noise from other strings.

In Example 2g, the same exercise is played on the second string. Here, the slide should be parallel to the strings and resting on most of them. Mute the surrounding strings to play this cleanly by resting the middle finger of the picking hand on the first string, and the thumb across the lower strings. Use the index finger to pluck the second string. This way it's impossible for any notes to ring out other than the one intended.

Example 2g:

The next example combines notes on the first and second strings. Here I use my thumb to mute the lower strings when playing on the high D string, and move the muting pattern over when changing string.

Example 2h:

Here's a lick that combines open and fretted notes with the slide. The difficulty here is getting used to the pressure required to make the notes sound clearly. Too little pressure and you'll get a buzz; too much and you'll be fretting the note on the fingerboard.

Example 2i:

Finally, here's a similar idea, but playing chords across four strings.

Example 2j:

Spend some time moving around the neck and playing random notes, making sure they're in tune and sound clean. The skill you're learning here is helping to develop a feel for how much pressure is needed to get a good, clear note out of the guitar. It can take time, but it's important that this feels automatic.

Let's turn these exercises into a Delta-style riff. Remember, Delta songs were built around riffs like these that repeated for many bars (measures) without many chord changes or variation. It was very much a vocal style and the guitar simply provided a harmonic "bed" for the lyrics.

At first this might seem confusing, but when broken down, you'll notice that there's a driving eighth note rhythm being played, and the chords fit around the open, 5th and 7th frets (the I, IV and V respectively).

To make it sound more musical, I've added a D chord at the 12th fret and a bluesy chord at the 3rd fret when playing on the D chord. This isn't treated as a new chord, but used to add some melodic shape to the example.

Example 2k:

This next example is based on one of the many variations of an eight-bar blues. As the 12-bar hadn't become the norm yet, there was so standard form for a blues – it wasn't uncommon to find 11-bar blues progressions – the chords just tended to follow wherever the vocal led.

Here I've opted for a simple I, IV, V progression where the I is played for four bars, before moving to the IV, V and I for a bar each.

To keep you on your toes I've added a walk-up from the 2nd to the 5th fret in the fourth bar of the repeat. Small details like this can turn something that sounds like an exercise into something resembling music!

Example 2l:

These two riffs were very basic and lacking a bit of finesse. In the next two chapters we'll look more at how to slide between notes cleanly and add the all-important vibrato.

Chapter Three – Sliding Between Notes

Now we've looked at the basics of fretting notes with the slide, we need to get to grips with the mechanics involved in sliding between notes.

It's important to keep applying pressure with the slide as you shift from one note to another. Don't squeeze the neck with your thumb, as the movement up and down the neck requires the whole arm to move, not just the wrist or finger.

Here's an example where I play a barred chord at the 3rd fret and slowly slide it up to the 12th. This slide can be played at any speed, but for technique practice, begin slowly and get used to the pressure required on the string to keep the note even. This example highlights one of the more nuanced aspects of slide guitar and shows how standard notation can be lacking when describing it. There's no way to indicate quickly you should slide, so use the audio recording as a guide to how it should sound.

Example 3a:

In the following single note lick, I slide between the notes quite quickly. Scalar ideas like this are common among slide players. The slide lends itself to playing lines that move up and down one string, rather than across many strings.

Example 3b:

Here's a similar idea, but one that makes bigger shifts around the neck and has notes going both up and down.

Example 3c:

The next example begins with a *grace note* – a quick note played just before the main note. In this case, the 10th fret is played, followed by an immediate slide up to the 12th. Grace notes are a great way to add expression and note articulation.

Example 3d:

To demonstrate how grace notes can bring a melody to life, here's a melody played without any articulation. This example has a gospel hymn feel to it – something that will have been common in the Delta at the time.

Example 3e:

Open D

Now here is the same melody with added grace notes to make it considerably more expressive.

Example 3f:

Open D

Slides can be used in a similar way to bending fretted notes. They allow us to start taking advantage of the microtonal options offered by a slide.

When notating these in tab, I'll use the bend symbol for illustration purposes, but we are using the slide to raise the pitch of the note. In the following example, play the 3rd fret, and then gradually slide the note so that it's a little sharp. This creates an authentic bluesy quality.

Example 3g:

Here's another idea with those bluesy slide bends played on several strings. Focus on keeping the muting as tight as possible at first, but then just go for it when playing and let some of the notes ring out.

Example 3h:

Another common sound you'll hear from any slide player is a wild slide from below into a note or chord. This is slightly different to a grace note, as the pitch you are sliding from isn't specified and may begin anywhere on the neck.

In the following example, strike the strings with the slide anywhere low on the neck and slide up to the 12th fret.

Example 3i:

Open D

Here's a melody at the low end of the neck that slides up to the 12th fret. After repeating this idea three times, the lick ends by sliding into an A Major chord at the 7th fret.

Example 3j:

Open D

These subjects will be revisited in much more detail throughout the book, but the examples in this section will help you get the fundamentals of the style down, so that musical ideas can be fully formed later.

Now, let's jump into the wonderful subject of vibrato.

Chapter Four – Vibrato

The word *vibrato* comes from the Italian word for vibrate and refers to any variation of pitch applied to a note. As a tool, vibrato helps to give a performer a way of adding personal expression to a note, and the importance of this can't be understated.

On an instrument such as piano, vibrato isn't an option and every note is mechanically in tune (assuming you have a good piano tuner!). With slide guitar, however, it's easy to play notes that are slightly out of tune – and a note that is slightly out is often much worse than a wrong note. One of the benefits of vibrato on slide guitar is that any minor pitching inconsistencies are masked.

So far we've been working on playing notes with no vibrato and there is a good reason for this: our aim is always to apply vibrato to a *good note*, not use it to hide the fact that we can't find the note we're aiming for!

Think of the notes you play as your speech, and the vibrato as the accent you use. Other people may use the same words as you, but the way in which *you* say them is unique. Similarly, you will develop your own style of vibrato that is unique to you; your calling card.

The technique used to apply vibrato is the same as sliding up and down the neck, but this time limited to a smaller area.

In Example 4a I begin with a full chord without vibrato then, as the note progresses, I begin subtly shaking my arm from left to right, gradually moving it wider as the note continues. This isn't the way all vibrato should take shape, but it's a good way to begin practising and understanding the technique.

Example 4a:

Here's a riff-based idea that begins on the lower part of the neck with a bluesy bend at the 3rd fret. It then slides up to the 12th fret on the higher strings with some wild vibrato. Playing something like this without the vibrato would sound sterile. In fact, after hearing these types of ideas *with* vibrato, the ideas in the previous chapters may sound a little off!

Example 4b:

Open D

D
```
      1/4                                    1/4
        12   (12)   12                          12   (12)
        12   (12)   12                          12   (12)
        12   (12)   12                          12   (12)
0—0—3—0—12   (12)   12            0—0—3—0—12   (12)
0—0—3—0                          0—0—3—0
0—0—3—0                          0—0—3—0
```

To demonstrate this, I've rerecorded Example 2n, but added a lyrical vibrato on the longer notes. Now it's starting to sound like real music.

Example 4c:

Open D

D7
```
—10–12——10——9———7—5——5—9—5–7———10–12——10——9———7—5——5—9—5–7—
```

Vibrato is an extremely difficult subject to cover in text form, as it's hard to conceptualize and demonstrate. In fact, it's often overlooked even when learning by ear. When describing vibrato to students, I find it best to help people to visualise it.

The following diagrams demonstrate this idea. The straight line represents the intended pitch, and the wavy line shows how the vibrato looks around the pitch.

This first diagram illustrates how vibrato sounds when played with the fingers on guitar. It's not possible to lower the pitch below the note you're fretting, so the vibrato rises above the note, then returns to pitch, and the pattern continues.

On the other hand, if vibrato was applied using a tremolo arm, the pitch would dip, then return.

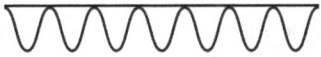

When playing with a slide, however, it's possible to apply vibrato that goes both *above* and *below* the main pitch, which might look something like this.

When you listen to a great singer, you'll notice that the voice tends to dip below the pitch before settling, then goes a little over the pitch before repeating. Imitating this using a slide results in an extremely musical vibrato that "surrounds" the note, without abandoning the vocal-like quality we hear from great soul singers, for instance.

In the following example, I demonstrate the difference between these vibratos. It's subtle, so it may take a while to really spot the difference.

Example 4d:

So far we have only scratched the surface of what's possible. There are many variables at play in vibrato and it's impossible to discuss each eventuality. We've looked at how vibrato can be used to *surround* the pitched note. How wide and fast our vibrato should be depends on the musical context in which it's being used.

Adding vibrato also comes down to taste. Some players have a naturally wide, slow vibrato, while others use a narrower, fast vibrato. Some will only apply vibrato to longer, sustained notes, while others apply a frantic vibrato to every note! It's all about experimentation and finding what you like the sound of.

These concepts aren't something I constantly think about when playing – it's a technique I practised in isolation until it became automatic. Now, vibrato is something I add to notes when I feel it's needed. The main thing is to focus on how *musical* your vibrato sounds. Listen to the great players and try to sound more like them.

Chapter Five – Open Tuning Scales

One of the quickest ways to learn an open tuning is to understand how each string functions in relation to the chord the guitar is tuned to. This makes it easy to transpose riffs and licks into new keys.

In open D tuning, the guitar is tuned to a D Major chord that contains the notes D (the root), F# (the 3rd) and A (the 5th). We can view the note on each open string according to its interval in relation to the root:

6th string D = Root

5th string A = 5th

4th string D = Root

3rd string F# = 3rd

2nd string A = 5th

1st string D = Root

Here's that information displayed in notation and tab, with the interval indicated above the notation.

Example 5a: (Notes at 12th fret are identical to notes on open string)

D Major

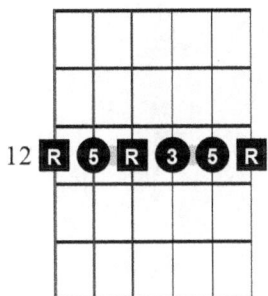

Playing the open strings or placing the slide directly over the 12th fret allows you to access all the "safe" notes of the chord. But what other notes can we add to this diagram to make music?

With a bit of knowledge about which scales best create the sound of the Delta blues, we can start to piece together a "map" of notes on the guitar that shows the best notes to use in our playing. This map can be used to construct riffs, licks and fills, and as the basis for your own song writing and improvisation.

Early Delta pioneers were probably not thinking about scales, but if we reverse-engineer their music we find that most of what they played was formed from what we now think of as the Mixolydian mode and the Blues scale.

Bear with me while we work though a little bit of music theory to create a useful map of the best notes to use when playing Delta blues. If you want to skip ahead, you'll see a diagram below that you can use immediately.

The D Blues Scale has the formula R b3 4 b5 5 b7 and contains the notes (D F G Ab A C)

D Mixolydian mode has the formula R 2 3 4 5 6 b7 and contains the notes (D E F# G A B C)

By combining these scales formulas we can create a hybrid-scale of intervals, all of which will work well over a D7 chord. They are:

R 2 b3 3 4 b5 5 6 b7 (D E F F# G Ab A B C).

All these notes sound great in the context of a Delta blues.

When we place some of these extra notes onto the guitar neck, something very interesting happens; they all lie two frets below the original "home" barre chord slide position.

D7

So, when playing a song in open D, we can place the slide at the 12th fret, and all the notes two frets lower are available as melodic embellishment when improvising or writing.

Here's a lick that uses this concept in its most basic form, using the 12th fret as "home" and sliding from two frets below.

Example 5b:

This concept makes it easy to outline chord changes, as demonstrated in the next example.

The "home" slide position can be moved onto any fret to outline any major chord. If you place it on the 7th fret you will play an A Major, and if you place it on the 5th fret you will outline a G Major chord.

In open D tuning, it's useful to remember that the root notes of chords on the sixth string are two frets above where they would be in standard tuning.

Example 5c:

Here's another lick that uses slides on the top three strings.

Example 5d:

The secret to using this pattern effectively is understanding that the upper slide position is "home" and the notes two frets lower are used embellish the chord. It's rarely pleasing to rest on the lower notes. Instead, they should be viewed as tension notes which are then resolved by sliding up two frets.

Obviously, this idea can easily be expanded by adding more notes above and below the home position, but it's incredible to see just how little the real Delta blues players needed to do that. There's plenty of music to be found just using this box pattern.

Melodic Notes in Open G Tuning

Now we've had a brief look at open D, let's jump to open G tuning and see if there's any common ground we can take advantage of.

As discussed in the first chapter, open G tuning from low to high is:

D G D G B D

G Major is made up of G (Root), B (3rd) and D (5th). The intervals of open G tuning are:

5 R 5 R 3 5

Here's that information displayed in notation and tablature.

Example 5e:

Again, all the notes of the chord are available as a barre with the slide at the 12th fret. Notice that the intervals are in a different order from open D tuning.

The interesting thing about open G tuning is that the lowest string isn't the root of the chord but rather the 5th. For this reason some players, such as Keith Richards of The Rolling Stones, have opted to remove the sixth string altogether.

Again, we can add some of the notes from the hybrid scale and once again, they appear two frets below the home chord.

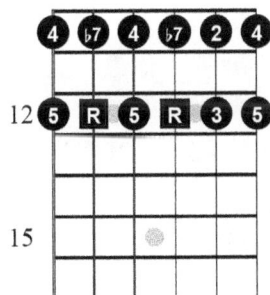

There are obvious similarities between open D and open G when compared in terms of their intervals. The two tunings are almost identical, but open D has an additional high note and open G has an additional low note.

I personally prefer open D over open G. It provides a little more low range (as the root is lower in pitch than in open G), and it also contains a root on the first string can give a great resolution to Delta blues melodies.

That said, it's easy to adapt to open G tuning quickly if we understand the intervals.

To demonstrate, here's the lick from Exercise 5d, but now played in open G tuning.

In the second bar, we don't have the option to jump up to the root on the high string, so this same note is played an octave lower on the third string.

Example 5f:

Let's extend the notes in open G tuning with another note from the hybrid scale, the 6th. The 6th is one tone higher than the 5th and sounds great when added above the highest note.

Let's also add the 4th above the 3rd on the second string.

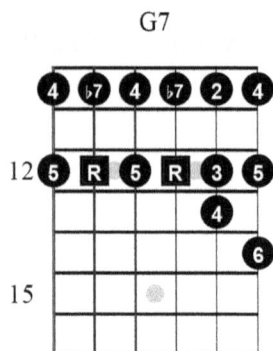

G7

```
        4  b7  4  b7  2  4
12      5  R   5  R   3  5
                    4
                       6
15
```

Here's a lick that uses these notes. As with earlier examples, the additional notes are used to create melodies that resolve to home notes of the chord on the 12th fret.

Example 5g:

Open G

```
T----------------12-12---------------------------------------------14-12------17--
A-------10-12-------------12-13--12----10-----------10-12---12-12--------12-------
B---12--------------------------------------12-----------------------------------
```

This idea can be expanded to build up a box patterns akin to those you probably visualize when playing fretted guitar in standard tuning. There is some benefit to this, but it's more common to play up and down one string rather than across the neck.

You may have noticed that we didn't really use the b3 or b5 of the hybrid scale in this chapter. These notes will come into their own as we start to explore the more traditional slide approach of one string playing.

Chapter Six – One String Scales

A useful way of getting to grips with slide technique and phrasing is to practise scales on a single string. While the ideas start off as exercises, they quickly become musical and applicable to Delta blues playing.

While this can be done anywhere, it's best to begin on the strings tuned to the root of the chord. Here's the D Major scale (D E F# G A B C#) played on the first string in open D tuning. Make sure you're playing directly over each fret and muting behind the slide. Play along with the audio track to check your intonation.

Example 6a:

Here's the same scale played using a little more slide phrasing and articulation.

Example 6b:

This same pattern will work on any string tuned to the root of the chord, so in open D, the same thing will work on the fourth string.

Example 6c:

The same fingering will also work on the sixth string.

Example 6d:

The Major scale is useful, but the Mixolydian mode is a scale that is suitable for playing Delta ideas over a Dominant 7 chord. It has the formula 1 2 3 4 5 6 b7.

Here's the D Mixolydian mode (D E F# G A B C) played on the first string. The only change from the Major scale is that the 7th degree of the Major scale is lowered by a semitone.

Example 6e:

This pattern can be played on each open D string. Here's the first and fourth string combined and played as octaves. This is a common approach among Delta blues players but don't forget to practise each string individually too.

Use the thumb and index finger to pluck the notes together in a pinching motion.

Example 6f:

Another common sound in Delta blues is the Major Pentatonic scale. This is a five-note scale consisting of the Root, 2 3 5 and 6. (D, E, F#, A and B in the key of D)

As it's missing that dark sounding b7 (C), the Major Pentatonic creates a softer sound that's heard in music all over the world.

Example 6g:

In the previous chapter, we built a hybrid scale that contained a b3 interval. It's common to add the b3rd (F) to this Major Pentatonic scale as a bluesy approach to the natural 3rd (F#).

Example 6h:

Here's a lick using the Major Pentatonic scale with the added b3. A common approach is to descend to the b3 (F) and move up to the natural 3 (F#). This makes the F# (a note that's in the chord) feel specifically targeted after playing the b3 (F) which isn't in the D Major chord.

Example 6i:

This difference between the darker b7th (C) and the sweeter 6th (B) is a subtle, but one that can be used to control the mood of the music.

For example, the following lick is the same as Example 6i, but plays the b7 instead of the 6 in bar three.

Play both of these ideas and compare the difference in sound. There are no right answers, it's all about building your own understanding of how your note choice affects the music.

Example 6j:

The Minor Pentatonic scale is very common in blues music. Like the Major Pentatonic scale, it is also a five-note scale, but with a different set of intervals. This time it's Root b3 4 5 b7 (D F G A C).

Here's that scale played on the first string. This scale "fits" a D Minor chord, but it's still a common choice on a major or dominant chord, where it has a rootsy, blues sound.

Example 6k:

It's common to add a quarter tone bend (often referred to as a "blues curl") to the b3rd in a blues. This puts the note somewhere between the F and F#, which is an important blues idiosyncrasy. It hints at the b3 to natural 3rd movement we discussed in Example 6i.

Play the scale with the added blues curl by moving the slide slightly up the neck towards the 4th fret after playing the 3rd. Don't go all the way to the 4th fret though, just hint at it.

Example 6l:

An important exercise you can practise with single-string scales will develop your control of *pull-offs* from notes fretted with the slide to an open string. The idea is to pull-off with the slide and sound the open string.

As the slide can't pull off from the note in the same way as your finger tip normally would, the secret is to flick the slide downwards off the string towards the floor.

Take this example slowly because getting this technique accurate will be extremely useful down the road. Listen to the audio so you know what sound you are aiming for.

Example 6l2:

While playing slide in open tunings is a lot easier and more common, many Delta players (including Robert Johnson) also played in standard tuning occasionally. All the ideas in this section can be applied to standard tuning too. For example, playing Example 6l in standard tuning will result in the E Minor Pentatonic scale.

Example 6m:

The Blues scale is a common scale created by adding a b5 to the Minor Pentatonic scale: 1 b3 4 b5 5 b7. The b5 was included in our hybrid scale in the previous chapter.

Here's the Blues scale played on the first string in open D tuning.

Example 6n:

The next lick uses the Blues scale. Listen out for the b5 at the end of the first bar. This Blind Willie Johnson style lick uses the b5 blues note to imitate what the voice is singing.

As you become more comfortable with the idea, hum along as you play. This will connect your ears and fingers, and aid your musical expression.

Example 6o:

Here's a second lick on the first string using notes of the D blues scale. The possibilities are endless!

Example 6o2

Come up with your own phrases using the D Blues scale on one string.

Next, I've written a lick inspired by Tampa Red. While there are fewer notes here, there are some rapid shifts from the 12th fret to the 3rd that need to be handled with care. You don't want to overshoot the slides as no amount of vibrato will cover that up.

Example 6p:

The final line in open D is a Bukka White-inspired lick that adds the open second string.

The hardest part comes in the second bar where we're required to slide from the 5th to the 7th fret, then to the 3rd fret before pushing that note slightly sharp. Again, a bend like this is created by moving the slide very slightly up the fretboard.

Listen to the audio recording and it will all make sense.

Example 6q:

With some open D vocabulary under your belt, let's look at some single-string open G lines too.

The first thing to get used to in open G is that the root note now sits at the 5th fret on the first string. This is great because you can now play the root note and add some expressive vibrato.

Example 6r:

The b3 is three frets above the root and the b7 is two frets below the root. These two notes are integral to the sound of the Minor Pentatonic scale and are extremely expressive.

Example 6s:

Sliding up to the 5th of the chord on the 12th fret is another strong, commonly heard sound in Delta blues. In the following example I move from the 5th to the b5 and back to really milk that powerful blues quality.

Example 6t:

Here's another idea that ascends the first string while sliding into each note. Listen closely to the recording as this melody is all about the slides rather than perfect intonation and accuracy.

Example 6u:

Finally, here's a lick in G Major that uses most of the notes at your disposal over the entire span of the octave. Take it slowly and experiment with the articulation to make it expressive and personal.

Example 6v:

As you continue through this book, you'll find many more examples of licks that move up and down a single string, and all of them are derived from the handful of scales covered in this chapter.

Keep adding more licks to your arsenal and get an idea of how you can categorize them in your mind. Using the blues note (b5th) makes a lick instantly unsettling. The 6th gives a lick a sweeter feel, compared to the b7th, which has a more serious vibe. This is just my opinion. Playing Delta blues is all about how these notes make *you* feel. If you keep exploring these sounds and listening to the early masters, you'll quickly develop a strong connection between your ears and fingers.

Chapter Seven – Open Position Playing

Having focused on playing up and down a single string, we will now look at playing across the strings. In the Delta blues, this approach is used to create riffs that last for a whole song, often using just one, or maybe two chords.

One of the most utilised areas of any open tuning is the area around the open position. Here is a diagram in the open position, showing some of the commonly used notes in this area.

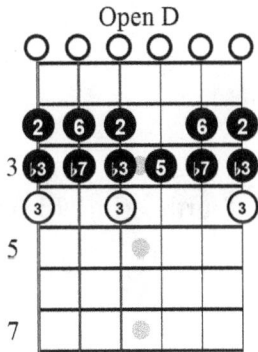

To move from an open string to a note fretted with the slide we have to place the slide down on the string. This can be a bit messy and create some unwanted noise unless you master the correct technique. It's a bit like playing a normal hammer-on, but the string is not pressed all the way down to the fret.

As with fretted guitar, pluck the open string, then lower the slide onto the string so that the new note sounds. Remember to place the slide directly over the fret and mute the strings behind it. Be firm, but not so hard that you cause the string to touch the fret wire.

This exercise is all about learning the amount of pressure required to sound the note clearly without pressing the string to the fingerboard. If you really struggle, you may want to consider having a new nut fitted that is a touch higher, or place a small shim under your current nut to raise the action.

In my picking hand, I use my thumb to play the 5th string, and my index finger on the 4th string. Alternating between these fingers allows you to mute strings more effectively if you need to.

Example 7a:

Here's the same idea, but this time hammering onto the 6th interval (B) on the fifth string to hint at that sweeter major pentatonic sound.

Example 7b:

The next example uses this hammer-on idea in a blues riff and adds a bluesy bend on the fourth string. Ideas like this often form driving rhythm patterns behind a vocal part, so dig in and let it ring!

Example 7c:

This idea can be repeated in a higher octave by moving it over to the second and first strings. I've turned the previous example into something that's more of a lead line by adding some melodic embellishment in the second and fourth bars and playing it on the higher strings

Example 7d:

The previous two ideas, and the lines in the rest of the chapter, are perfect to use as accompaniment to a solo vocal in the true Delta style. Of course, you can use them in regular blues playing or in a band, but the authentic approach is to sing a melody over a riff and play a lick in the gaps between each line.

The next line adds pull-offs. These are tricky with a slide because there's no real way to pull off the string. Unlike a regular, fretted pull-offs, you can't just lift the slide off the string. The secret here is to *flick up* the string as you leave it, to sound the open string a little louder.

Example 7e:

Again, we can move this idea over to the second and first strings to create something more akin to a solo.

Example 7f:

Here's another lick using bluesy bends on the b3rd on both the first and fourth strings.

Example 7g:

When you begin to dig in with the thumb pick or thumb, you will quickly find that hitting more than one string often works well when playing slide, because all the strings are tuned to the same chord.

Example 7h is based on the previous idea, but adds some grinding double stops on the fourth and third strings, along with a slide up to the 12th fret.

Example 7h:

Here's another example based on the same riff with some quicker grace note slides. Ideas like this are difficult to express perfectly in standard notation, so listen to the audio to hear the nuances.

When recording this lick, I began by playing it as cleanly as possible, but as time went on, I found it sounded better when it was given some attitude and when the notes were allowed to ring out along with a few extra strings.

This lick has such attitude because it includes the b5th (Ab on the 2nd fret, third string). The interplay between the b5th and the 5th (open second string) gives it a particularly dark sound.

Example 7i:

The following example uses several of the notes around the open position, along with double stops for a more aggressive sound.

Example 7j:

Here's another example, this time a little longer. It combines a single string idea with notes added in the open position.

This is the approach many slide players take, as playing across the strings in other positions can be awkward. Using the open strings means you can let any note ring out and it's going to be in key since the guitar is tuned to a chord.

Example 7k:

As you continue to explore the style of the Mississippi Delta legends, you'll find the same melodic ideas coming up again and again, regardless of tuning. This is due to the similarities in the tunings that we discussed in Chapter Five.

Here's a scale box that you could think of when tuning to open G. Notice how similar it is to the open D tuning box I showed you earlier.

Open G

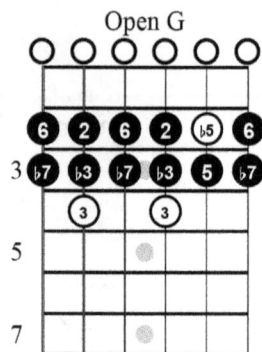

With the guitar tuned to open G, we quickly notice that the licks don't feel too different to the ones in open D. In the following lick, the most notable addition to the diagram is the root note (G) played at the 5th fret on the first string. This high-octave root allows us to add vibrato to that note – something we couldn't do if it was played on the open string, like in open D tuning.

Example 7l:

Here's another lick that uses triplets for a faster, more driving effect. Learn this one slowly as the position shifts are tricky at speed.

Example 7m:

The next line crosses five strings in the open position. Pay careful attention to the rhythm in bar two which features more syncopation (playing notes on the upbeat) to grab the listener.

Example 7n:

You can also add double stops for a bit more aggression. As always, listen closely to the recording to get a feel for the articulation and vibrato.

Example 7o:

Example 7p incorporates a double stop idea at the 3rd fret.

Example 7p:

To finish the chapter, learn this tricky 1/16th note idea using a fast slide between the 5th and b5 on the second string. This can be played a little "rough around the edges", with each note ringing out, or a little more cleanly by adding more muting.

Example 7q:

Don't be afraid to experiment and combine these ideas to create your own phrases. The blues is about expressing yourself, even if that expression comes from a limited pool of notes. The only way to be completely free to do that is to exhaust these concepts and find what works and what sounds good.

When you're comfortable with these ideas, move on to the next chapter where I've written two solos using these ideas on a Delta blues tune.

Chapter Eight – Saint Louis Blues

In this chapter you'll learn a full 12-bar solo in open G tuning, based very loosely on the 1914 W. C. Handy blues standard, *Saint Louis Blues*. Over the years, this song became common in the repertoire of jazz pioneers like Louis Armstrong, Count Basie, Glenn Miller and Bessie Smith, although it's nothing more than a 12-bar blues in D.

Consisting of just the I, IV and V chords in the key of D, the first step is to learn the rhythm guitar part.

To keep it simple, I've written the rhythm guitar in standard tuning, so the chord voicings will be familiar to you, and you'll be able to play it more easily with a friend who isn't a slide guitar/open tuning specialist. Of course, you can play the chords with the slide in open D tuning if you wish.

Example 8a:

While the song is in the key of D, the soloist is actually tuned to open G. This seems counterintuitive at first, but the reason is so that the soloist can use the note B on the second string when the chord changes to G Major. (The B note is the 3rd of G Major – a very strong note to target on the chord).

Learn this solo slowly and listen carefully to the recording to get an idea of the feel. It should sound bluesy, not robotic. Bend the notes to taste and add vibrato when it feels right.

Example 8b:

Here's one another 12-bar solo in open G tuning, this time based more around the fourth string (D).

The defining aspect of this solo is the repeating ascending chromatic parts. This is a great example of how this style of playing doesn't need to be perfectly in tune.

For example, in bar two we move up chromatically from fret 4 to fret 7. The authentic way to play a lick like this isn't to play precisely on each fret. Rather, we slide from 4 to 7 while picking the string four times.

Example 8c:

Once you've got this example under your fingers, work on playing the two solos back to back. As mentioned at the start of the chapter, examples like these are great fun to play with a friend, as the rhythm guitar part is something even a beginner could learn quite quickly.

When you're able to play this piece comfortably, your next port of call should be spending some time listening to the greats playing this song (Spotify has many different versions). The more idea you have about how an experienced musician plays over a tune like this, the more you'll be able to express yourself freely in your own playing.

Chapter Nine – Melodies And Bass

While Delta blues guitarists often stick to playing isolated melodies, solo guitar players often play both rhythm and lead guitar parts together. This approach is extremely common among acoustic guitarists who play without a slide. In open tuning with a slide, things become trickier.

To play rhythm and lead together you must develop independence between the thumb and the fingers of your picking hand.

We'll begin in open D tuning with a repeating quarter note on the sixth string. Use the thumb to play this note with a solid downstroke motion.

Example 9a:

When this becomes comfortable, the next step is to add a single note held over the top.

Slide up to the 12th fret on the first string and hold this note while adding vibrato. Keep playing the driving bass part with the thumb.

Example 9b:

This same exercise can be repeated with a three-note chord ringing on top. Use the index, middle and ring fingers to pluck the chord, while playing the bass note with the thumb.

To play this exercise cleanly, we have to be careful with the position of the slide. Here, we need to fret several strings while keeping the low string open. The slide cannot cover all six strings.

Example 9c:

Open D

Example 9d includes some *offbeat* notes. The first melody note is played in tandem with the bass using a pinching motion, then the melody note is repeated on its own.

To mix it up a little, I've also changed the melody slightly in each bar.

Example 9d:

Open D

When this begins to feel normal, alter the melody in the middle of the bar. In this example the melody note changes from D to C on the "&" of beat 2.

Example 9e:

Now that the right-hand mechanics have been introduced, you are free to add more notes with the slide to create a stronger melody.

The following example develops the previous idea into a descending melody.

Example 9f:

With this concept under your belt, it's possible to start creating some really musical ideas using just the notes of the D Minor Pentatonic scale over the driving bass part.

Example 9g:

The next example builds on this idea by playing the motif in bar one and shifting to an open position lick in the second bar.

Learning to keep these bass notes ringing out as you move across the strings takes time, so be patient.

Example 9h:

Developing this idea further, we can start to mix phrases played in the open position with notes that we slide up to. This puts us in Son House, *Dead Letter Blues* territory. Ideas like this sound best when played fast and loose.

Example 9i:

This final idea combines notes in the open position with added vibrato at the 12th fret.

Example 9j:

It's also possible to play an 1/8th note pattern with the thumb, as shown in the following example. Ideas like these are most commonly played with a swing feel.

Example 9k:

As with the 1/4 note bass pattern, it's possible to have one melody note ring out while the thumb plays a steady bass part.

Example 9l:

When you add 1/8th note melodies, each note is played simultaneously with a bass note in a pinching motion. To demonstrate this, here's an idea that uses open strings and the 12th fret played with the slide.

Example 9m:

Here's a similar rhythm, with a melody played on the first string using notes of the D Blues scale against a driving 1/8th note bass part.

Example 9n:

As with the 1/4 note bass part, it's worthwhile to practise open position licks with these bass parts. When listening to the audio, you'll notice that I play the slides quite slowly on this lick – they just feel right that way!

Example 9o:

Another great idea is to split the melody and bass in a triplet rhythm.

Example 9p:

Here's the same idea, but notated more correctly with an upper and lower voice. This is a convention in two-part music where the bass line is written with downward stems and the melody is written with upward stems.

Example 9q:

The following example features melody notes played on both the strong beats and these offbeat triplets. This looks more complicated than it is, as long as you've mastered the previous example, so listen to the audio to get the timing.

Example 9r:

The following two-bar phrase combines open-string licks, position shifts and off-beat triplets.

This is probably one step beyond what you'll hear in authentic Delta blues playing, but it's great for your creativity and technical ability to work on ideas like this. Anything simpler will be a walk in the park when you can play this example!

Example 9s:

This final idea will prepare you for the blues solos in the final chapters and introduces an alternating bass pattern played by the thumb.

In open D tuning, both the fourth and sixth strings are tuned to D, so alternating between them gives a nice driving octave pattern as a framework for our melodies.

Example 9t:

These types of alternating bass patterns are common in the country fingerstyle genre (check out my book *Country Fingerstyle Guitar* for more!) and must be practised until they're completely automatic in the thumb before you start adding melodies over the top.

Example 9u combines the alternating thumb pattern with a descending scale on the first string. Phrases such as these are the basis of classics like Blind Willie Johnson's *Dark Was The Night, Cold Was The Ground*.

Example 9u:

This technique can be also used in rhythm guitar patterns, as shown in the next example.

Keep the alternating pattern in the thumb, but now add the second and first strings on the 1st and 2nd beats respectively. These chords are played with a pinching motion between the thumb and index finger.

Example 9v:

When you add notes on the up-beat, you start to create something that sounds engaging and complex without doing much hard work.

This example is the same as the previous one, but adds an additional plucked note on the & of beat 3.

Example 9w:

Open D

These picking concepts could be expanded almost infinitely, but I don't want to stray too far from the subject at hand. Let's move on now you have the basics under your fingers.

With these rhythmic picking ideas on one chord nailed, let's explore some licks that outline the chord changes of the blues.

Chapter Ten – Changing Chords

When playing in an open tuning, the guitar naturally lends itself to playing in the key of the tuning – i.e. it's very easy to play in the key of D on a guitar in open D tuning. Of course, songs don't stay on the same chord forever, so we need to learn to play and solo over other chords too. Overcoming this hurdle is one of the biggest challenges you'll come up against in this style.

Before we get into changing chords, let's take a quick look at playing in different keys. For example, how do we approach playing in the key of E if the guitar is tuned to open D? Imagine getting on stage to find that the singer can only sing in E and you don't have time to retune your whole guitar.

One way to approach playing in the key of E while tuned to open D is simply to move your perspective of where the "home" position is. E is one tone (two frets) above D, so instead of the open strings and the 12th fret forming the tonic chord, you now view "home" at the 2nd and 14th frets instead.

Example 10a:

This concept opens up other options too. With the home position at the 2nd fret you can, for example, play notes below the barre that you couldn't access before. As the following example demonstrates, this results in some unique ideas that would be impossible in the key of D.

Example 10b:

The drawback with this approach is that any open string licks you had in your arsenal are now unavailable. In the key of D, all the open strings were "strong" notes, but in the key of E they are "weak". Not "wrong", because technically they are all in key, but they don't sound as good.

There is an easy solution though, and that's to use a capo. Placing a capo at the second fret puts the whole guitar into the key of E and makes all the open-string licks you've already learned available again.

Example 10c:

Here's Example 7i, but now played with a capo at the 2nd fret to change the lick from the key of D to the key of E.

In this example, sliding up twelve frets with the capo at the 2nd fret, means you're actually playing at the 14th fret. If you are playing a resonator guitar where the neck joins the body at the 12th fret, this can be awkward, so sometimes you'll have to adapt your vocabulary accordingly.

Example 10d:

Key changes aside, most Delta blues is formed from just three chords, the I, the IV and the V (D, G and A in the key of D). As each chord is often played for an extended time, we can adjust our thinking to treat each chord almost as if it's in a different key.

Generally speaking, in Delta blues style, each chord is treated as if it's a dominant 7 chord.

The simplest way to deal with these chord changes is to use the strength of the open tuning, and to treat each chord change as a new "home" position.

In open D tuning:

- The open strings / 12th fret barre forms the (I) chord, D Major

- A 5th fret barre forms the IV chord, G Major

- The 7th fret barre forms the V chord, A Major

Example 10e:

The beauty of this system is that the concept of the "home barre chord" works perfectly for each chord. The notes that work over the G Major and A Major chords form the same pattern on the neck as the D Major position we've discussed at length. You can see this in the following diagrams.

The following example uses a lick on the D chord for four bars, then transitions to the G Major (IV) chord by moving to a barre chord at the 5th fret. This is an easy way to outline the chord change and it works very well.

Example 10f:

The same approach can be used for the final four bars of the blues to outline the V chord (A Major) at the 7th fret, and the IV chord (G Major) at the 5th fret, before returning to the open position for the I chord (D Major).

Example 10g:

In the following example, I've written a simple melodic lick moving between A, G and D, using the simple pattern presented in example 10f.

Example 10g1

Here's another idea based around the same concept. Ideas like this are used often, and may appear fairly basic, but they're extremely effective at adding something interesting to a solo or rhythm part.

Example 10g2

This is a common approach to navigating the blues. In Chapter Thirteen you will see this concept in use in the *Guitar Rag* example piece, for any chord that isn't played in the open position.

While shifting positions is a great strategy, it's important to have some single string and open position options at your disposal for the chord changes.

The following example plays an ascending hybrid scale in D, then the same idea in G at the 5th fret.

Example 10h:

Now try this lick that moves between G Major and D Major and uses these two patterns in a more musical manner.

Example 10i:

Here's a different lick, using the same concept of a single string scale for both the G and D chords.

Example 10j:

Another benefit of seeing the home position of each chord in different places on the neck is that you can play notes behind the slide which would be impossible in the open position.

In the following example, I play notes behind the G and A barres (at the 5th and 7th frets).

Example 10k:

Now let's add notes around the barre position on other strings, as covered in Chapter Five.

Here's a lick repeated on G and A chords. Remember, these licks are very logical when you see the barre chord position as home.

Example 10l:

In the context of a blues, it's possible to create some melodic ideas without using much material. These ideas work because each chord is surrounded closely by the melody.

Example 10m:

With those ideas under your fingers, it's time to explore some open position soloing for each chord.

The next example gives you four short open-string licks for G7 in open D tuning.

Example 10n:

Of course, you should explore this concept further to develop your own language, so here's full neck diagram that shows the "home" position of G Major with the notes available in the open position.

I've also ascended the neck on the first string to help you explore the higher range of the guitar. Strong chord notes are shown in black and the tension notes are shown in white. The rule of thumb is normally to resolve from a tension note to a strong chord tone.

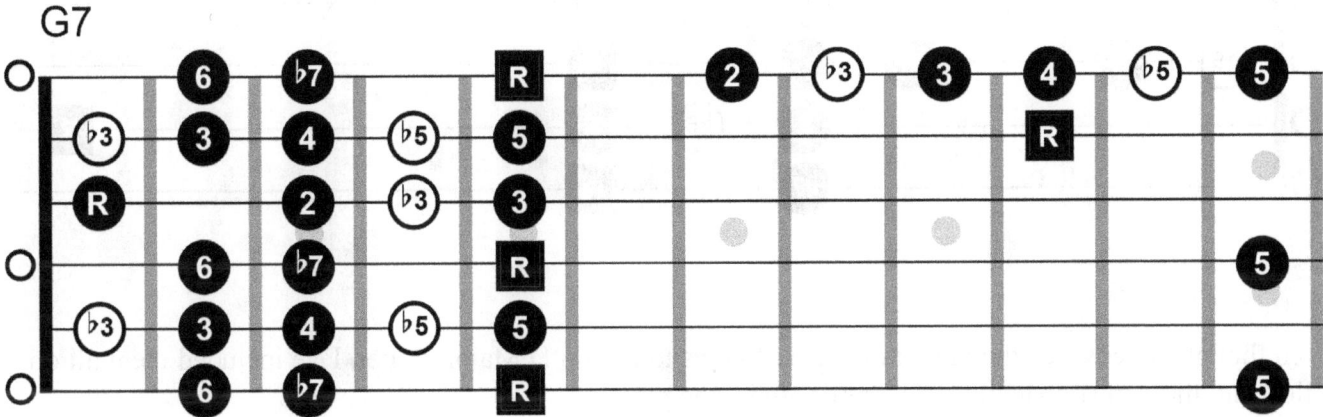

Now here are some open string licks for the V chord (A7) in open D tuning. The root note is on the second string and these licks focus their melodies around that point.

Example 10o:

Again, explore this idea on your own to develop a personal language. Below I've mapped out the "home" position of A Major – this time on the 7th and 5th frets – and added the available notes in the open position. Once again, the white notes are tension notes that should be resolved to the black chord tones.

A7

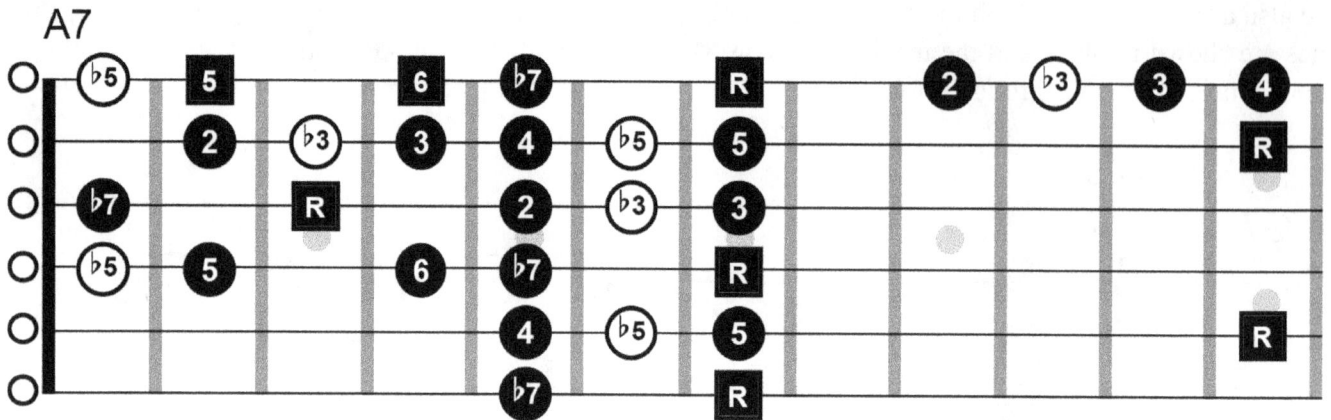

Even though we covered the layout of the best notes to use on D Major earlier, I've included them all on the following diagram so that all the diagrams are in one place.

D7

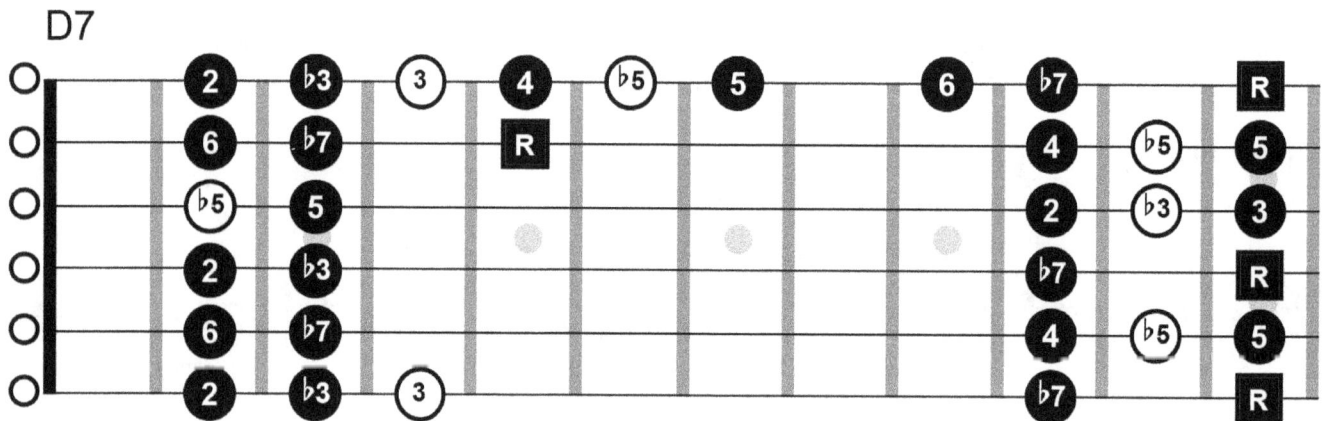

These positions will be exploited fully in the solos chapter at the end of the book, so get familiar with them now as you'll need them soon!

It's important you understand that whether you're in open D or open G tuning, the I chord will always be formed from the open strings, the IV chord will always be played at the 5th fret, and the V chord will always be played at the 7th fret.

To show you what I mean, let's look at how this works in open G tuning. The I, IV and V chords in the key of G are G Major, C Major and D Major respectively.

Example 10p:

We can explore this further by examining a 12-bar blues idea that outlines the chord changes by shifting between the open, 5th and 7th frets.

Example 10q illustrates a riff-based idea around the all-important open position.

Example 10q:

Example 10r begins by targeting the IV chord (C) on the 5th fret, then plays a lick based heavily around this position before moving back down to the open position to outline the chord change back to G.

Example 10r:

The V chord, D Major is played at the 7th fret. The following example targets "home" again with a barre chord shape on beat one, then decorates it with a riff using the box pattern you're familiar with by now.

The final four bars move down through the V, IV and I chords before returning to the V chord (this is called a *turnaround*). Notice how the changes are clearly outlined by moving the home position on each chord.

Example 10s:

Go back over this section slowly, and really pay attention to these "home" positions. This is an integral part of learning to change chords fluently when playing slide. Once you get your head around the idea that playing slide often means treating a barred fret as "home", you'll take to learning licks and patterns much faster.

Chapter Eleven – Fretting Notes Using Fingers

The Delta blues style goes beyond just playing notes with the slide. You also need to become comfortable playing notes with your spare fingers, whilst wearing the slide.

I wear my slide on my pinkie finger as it fits my particular style of playing best, but you can use it on the ring finger too. Experiment with what's most comfortable for you, and work through the examples in this chapter to find the best way to execute them.

One of the most common blues riffs is easily executed with just one finger in the open position in either open D or open G tuning.

Use the index finger to play the fretted note in the first example, while wearing the slide on your chosen finger. This can be played either straight or with a shuffle feel.

You'll see in the tablature below that there is no way to know whether the fretted note is played with your finger or with the slide. Unfortunately, this is one of the drawbacks of music notation. Sometimes you just have to use some common sense and your ears to figure out which notes are fretted with the fingers and which are fretted with the slide.

Example 11a:

This example begins with the same blues riff, then moves up the neck to play a melody with the slide.

Example 11b:

Still in open D tuning, let's try that riff on a G Major chord. The following example does not use a slide, but you should still be wearing it!

Example 11c:

An easy note to add to the open D riff is the C at the 3rd fret on the fifth string. The C is the b7 of D and creates a bluesy D7 sound.

Example 11d:

A similar idea adds some movement between the I (D) and IV (G) chords. Play the D riff for three bars and the D7 sound in bar four. This helps pull the chord progression to the G chord in bar five.

Example 11e:

G ... **D**

```
TAB (bars 5-8):
5—5—7—7—5—5—7—7   5—5—7—7—5—5—7—7   0—0—2—2—0—0—2—2   0—0—2—2—3—3—2—2
5—5—5—5—5—5—5—5   5—5—5—5—5—5—5—5   0—0—0—0—0—0—0—0   0—0—0—0—0—0—0—0
```

Let's add the V chord (A) using the same pattern at the 7th fret to complete the blues pattern.

Example 11f:

Open D

D ... **D7**

```
TAB (bars 1-4):
                                                      0—0—0—0—0—0—0—0—0—0—0—0
                                                      0—0—0—0—0—0—0—0—0—0—0—0
0—0—2—2—0—0—2—2   0—0—2—2—0—0—2—2   0—0—2—2—0—0—2—2   3—3—3—3—3—3—3—3—3—3—3—3
0—0—0—0—0—0—0—0   0—0—0—0—0—0—0—0   0—0—0—0—0—0—0—0   0—0—0—0—0—0—0—0—0—0—0—0
```

G ... **D**

```
TAB (bars 5-8):
5—5—7—7—5—5—7—7   5—5—7—7—5—5—7—7   0—0—2—2—0—0—2—2   0—0—2—2—3—3—2—2
5—5—5—5—5—5—5—5   5—5—5—5—5—5—5—5   0—0—0—0—0—0—0—0   0—0—0—0—0—0—0—0
```

A ... **G** ... **D**

```
TAB (bars 9-12):
7—7—9—9—7—7—9—9   5—5—7—7—5—5—7—7   0—0—2—2—0—0—2—2   0—0—2—2—3—3—2—2
7—7—7—7—7—7—7—7   5—5—5—5—5—5—5—5   0—0—0—0—0—0—0—0   0—0—0—0—0—0—0—0
```

There are many ways to decorate these basic riffs to outline the sound of the blues. Here's another voicing that can be used in place of the IV (G) chord in bars five and six.

This voicing is much harder to play as it requires the use of three fingers. This is one where the slide being on the pinky will come in handy!

Example 11g:

Here's a three-finger voicing that can be used to play the V chord (A Major) in open D tuning. Remember, you should still be wearing your slide!

Example 11h:

We can use the spare fretting fingers to play single notes that punctuate open position riffs, as this *Death Letter Blues*-inspired riff demonstrates.

Example 11i:

Open D

We can also use fretted notes to play a stereotypical blues turnaround, as demonstrated in the following *Crossroads*-inspired lick.

Use the first finger of the fretting hand to move downwards chromatically on the fifth string, before shifting up to the V chord (A) on the 7th fret with the slide.

Example 11j:

Open D

The next example has a similar pattern, but mixes it up by adding the second string to the triplet part and adding descending quarter notes in the bass part. Turnarounds like this were very common in the playing of Robert Johnson.

Example 11k:

Open D

Example 11l:

Open D

Depending on the tuning you're in, this same pattern can be exploited elsewhere. In open D, both the fifth and second strings are tuned to A, so the descending bass note that was played on the fifth string could be moved over to the second string for an alternative approach.

Double-stops are also a nice way to add some variety to your playing. They sound great when you add in the slide for fills.

To execute these 6th intervals, you must use the index and middle fingers of the fretting hand while keeping the slide out of the way.

Example 11m:

This idea can also be adapted to help you play more interesting turnaround licks, this time with descending 6ths on the third and fifth strings.

Example 11n:

Playing these 6th intervals can be tricky, because the note patterns change as you move up the neck. Octaves are an easier option for the aspiring slide player. As the first and fourth strings are tuned to D, and the second and fifth strings are tuned to A, playing two notes on the same fret on these strings allows you to play an octave easily.

Example 11k showcases these patterns on both strings. As with the previous example, use the first and second finger to fret them.

Example 11o:

You can also play octaves between the fourth and sixth strings. Play the following lick to master the string changes while playing octaves.

Example 11p:

One final use of the fingers is to play single note melodies with techniques like hammer-ons and pull-offs. While it's possible to play these with a slide, fretting these notes normally will always give you accurate intonation and help you play cleaner notes, as playing them with the slide can cause adjacent strings to sound.

The following lick sounds a little cleaner when hammering onto the 2nd fret with the index finger of the fretting hand, rather than the slide. The slide is then used to play a bluesy bend on the fourth string.

Example 11q:

There really is no end to the possibilities here and they go way beyond the scope of a book focused on Delta blues slide playing. Playing slide blues is about the slide becoming an extension of your body. A big part of that is learning to use the fingers independently while wearing the slide.

It's worthwhile grabbing any resources on playing fingerstyle blues and learning to play the licks and phrases in your chosen tuning while wearing the slide. Developing this level of dexterity is an excellent use of your time as you'll to make the slide contribute to, rather than hinder, your blues vocabulary.

Chapter Twelve – Solo Blues

With all the basic Delta techniques understood, there's no better way to practise fluency than by learning a full solo.

I've composed this tune in open G, so you can see just how similar these tunings are. While open D can be a lot of fun, having the I chord sounding so low can be a drag. Open G brings a nice change of pace as the I chord is now a 4th higher and you have the notes in the box pattern available below the chord.

Here's a full neck diagram of the notes in open G tuning showing their relationship to the tonic G Major chord. This map combine the notes of the G Mixolydian mode (G A B C D E F) and the G Blues scale (G Bb C Db D F), to create a hybrid blues scale consisting of the intervals R 2 b3 3 4 b5 5 6 b7.

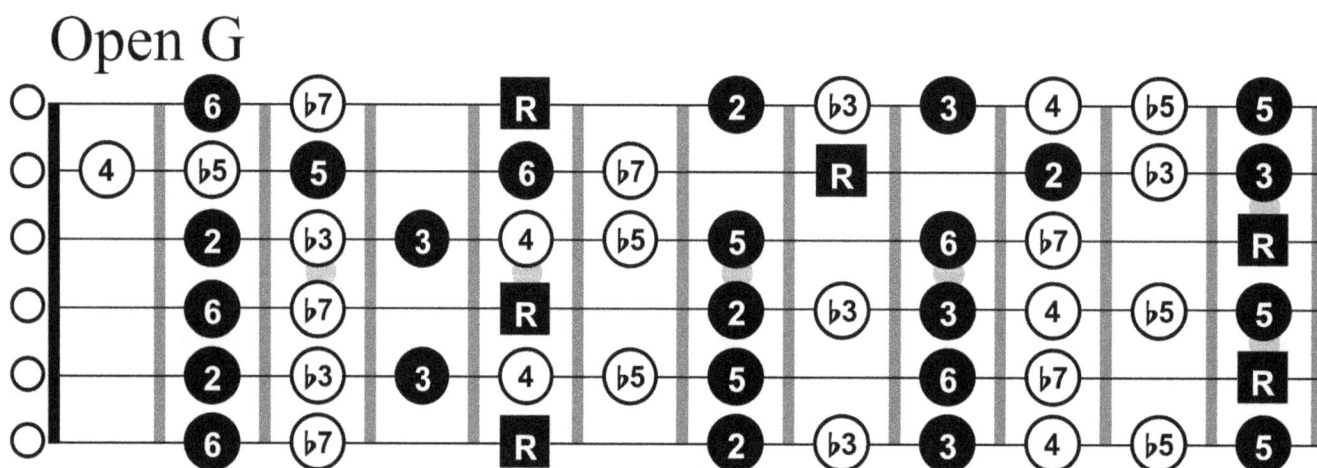

Open G

String										
○		6	b7		R		2	b3	3	4	b5	5
○	4	b5	5		6	b7		R		2	b3	3
○		2	b3	3	4	b5	5		6	b7		R
○		6	b7		R		2	b3	3	4	b5	5
○		2	b3	3	4	b5	5		6	b7		R
○		6	b7		R		2	b3	3	4	b5	5

While this diagram contains a lot of notes, remember that most of your playing will be based around the "home" position of G Major on the 12th fret, and the line of notes below that on the 10th fret. The other notes provide colour or tension to create more interesting melodies.

Notes such as the b3 and b5 should be used as passing notes and resolve to stronger ones. In the following piece, you'll gain most mileage out of focusing on the G Major Pentatonic scale (1 2 3 5 6).

Open G - G Major Pentatonic

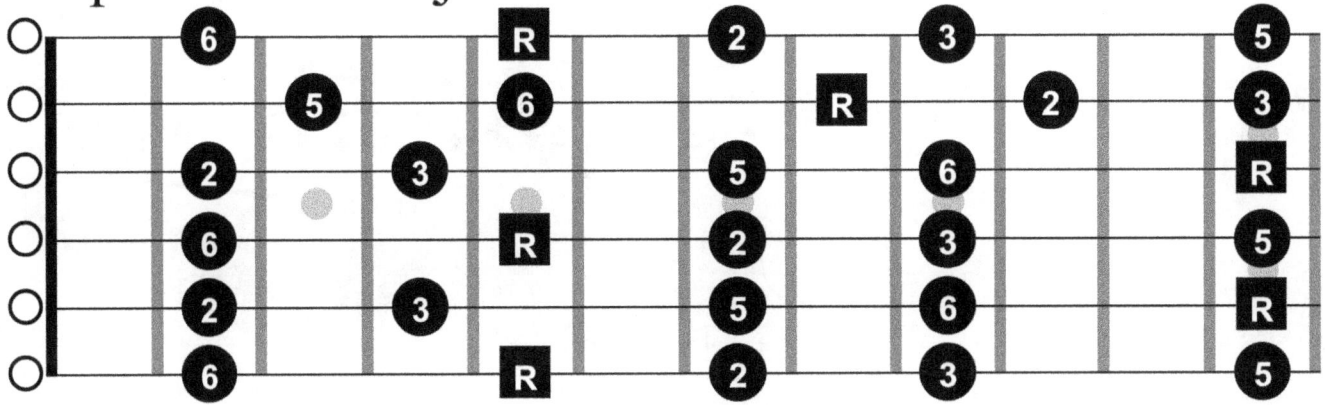

Blues Solo Breakdown

Learn the following sections individually before joining them together into one complete piece.

The first four bars all outline a G Major chord using a barre at the 12th fret and the first lick acts as an introduction to the twelve-bar form. To make things bluesy, move the double stop slides in bar three really slowly.

Example 12a:

The next four bars complete the introduction by hitting the V chord (D Major), then playing a classic turnaround to get you into the song.

In the first two bars, use your finger to play the 1st fret on the second string, and hammer from the open fourth string to the 2nd fret.

The turnaround lick can be tricky to play, as it requires fingers to fret notes while the top and bottom notes move in different directions. After playing the open G Major chord in bar three, the notes on the fourth string descend chromatically from the 3rd fret, while the notes on the second string ascend chromatically from the open string.

Example 12b:

The next riff forms a repeating figure that defines the first chorus and will take some patience to perfect. The slide on the sixth string and the open double stops are ideally played with a thumb pick, while the other notes are played with the fingers.

The notes with downward stems indicate that the bass notes should be played with the thumb. The up stems should be played with the fingers.

Learn this idea extremely slowly until it feels effortless, because a real Delta blues player would be able sing while playing a guitar part such as this.

Example 12c:

The following two bars continue the same feel with a repeating double stop played by the thumb, while altering the melody a little with a slide up to the 12th fret.

The final barre here can be tricky, as you need to let the open strings ring while playing the double-stop with the slide *and* applying vibrato. The final chord hints at an F Major triad over a G bass which creates a G7 sound.

Example 12d:

While you might expect the next two bars to rest on the IV (C Major), you'll find a slight variation in the progression, where the C Major chord is shifted up to Eb Major in the second bar. This creates a bluesy tension that pulls the progression back to the I chord.

The notes in beat 3 of the first bar should be fretted while the 4th beat is played with the slide.

When the song moves back to the G chord, use the thumb to pound away on the double-stop and keep the groove.

Example 12e:

Playing over the V chord (D Major) is achieved by moving to the 7th fret where a melody in octaves on the first and fourth strings decorate the chord.

We then move down a tone to the 5th fret to outline the IV chord (C Major), before ending on a turnaround lick which is played without the slide. The slide is used for the final chord at the 7th fret.

Example 12f:

On the second time through the progression, things are mixed up a bit with an open position riff which you should fret with your fingers, and added melodies with the slide for variation. All the double-stops are fretted with the finger and the single note melodies are played with the slide.

Example 12g:

Open G

On the IV chord (C Major) the fretted riff moves up to the 5th fret, which requires you to hold a two-fret barre with the first finger and to play the 7th fret with an additional finger. (As I place the slide on my pinkie finger, I'm using my ring finger, but any available finger will work).

The slide is again used to add single note melodies, offset against the riff.

Example 12h:

The final part of this solo continues with the theme of fretted chords and single note melodies played with the slide.

To outline the D Major chord, an open position C Major chord has been moved up two frets. This still gives us the D and F# notes, but with an open G string added, and results in a more colourful Dadd11 chord.

The solo ends with the same turnaround idea from the introduction, which now resolves to the I chord (G Major) at the 12th fret. Ending on the I chord like this gives the feeling that the music has come to an end.

Example 12i:

Once you have this entire piece under your fingers, you'll have a feel for how to play a twelve-bar blues in the Delta style. There's a fixed chord progression that's being followed, and as long as you know where you are in the chord progression you will be able to play some great music.

With the structure of the blues in mind, you could pick absolutely any lick from this book and use it in place of the licks that have been played in blues the tune above.

Nothing is set in stone. Delta slide guitar is about expressing yourself, so experiment and substitute the licks and lines you like the sound of into the tune. Write your own solos and discover the musical voice you have inside you.

Chapter Thirteen – Blues Rag

At the birth of the slide guitar movement was the *Guitar Rag*. Similar in style to the twelve-bar blues, the rag is a common chord progression used in early blues music. This tune includes a country-style thumb picked alternating bass line, so pay attention to the directions of the note stems so you know what should be played with the thumb, and what should be picked with the fingers.

For "Blues Rag", I've composed two full choruses of the progression and added an extra eight bars to end. The song is presented here one section at a time, but when you're comfortable with each section, you should play it as one complete piece as heard on the audio download.

While the twelve-bar blues in the previous chapter only included the I, IV and V chords, the ragtime progression also adds in the II chord (E) for some additional movement and shows an early jazz influence.

The first eight bars of the progression are predominantly based around the tonic chord of D, though there's a quick move to the V chord (A) in bar six, which creates a little movement without impacting the melody.

Throughout the first four bars, play the hammer-on with the first finger, then switch to the slide for the sustained notes on the first string.

When the chord moves to A Major in bar six, the octaves are fretted with the first and second fingers before using the slide on the 3rd fret bend in bar seven.

The most important part of the song is always the melody, so play the higher notes a little louder than the thumb part so they ring out clearly.

Example 13a:

Before tackling the next section as a complete part, it's worth getting to grips with the chord movement.

For this entire section, the slide barres across all six strings as it moves from chord to chord. The chord progression is G Major, D Major, E Major, A Major (IV I II V). The most authentic way to play this is to let the notes ring out and add a soft vibrato to help with the intonation.

Practise the isolated bassline before moving on.

Example 13b:

Playing the driving bass part means you can't really move the slide to play the melody, so all the melody notes need to fall under the slide.

When the chord changes to the open D, the slide is suddenly free to add a little more melody on the first string.

At the end of the progression the slide moves down from the 7th to the 6th fret on the final beat. This melody links back to the G Major chord at the 5th fret on the repeat.

Example 13c:

The next part of the melody is similar to the previous section, this time moving from E Major to A Major, then up to D Major in the final four bars.

This is a pleasing resolution as the melody can continue up the neck while the bass part moves down to the open strings.

Example 13d:

In essence, that's all there is to the tune, but that's the beauty of an uncomplicated song – it's possible to endlessly explore the tune and create variations that can be added to develop the music.

Here's a more challenging version of the first eight bars of the piece.

Example 13e:

Here's a more embellished version of the following section, this time with an open position lick in the third bar, and a slide into the E chord in the fifth bar.

You could play absolutely any lick in bar three; it's about adding something interesting to guide the listener into the D chord. Everything else is under the slide.

Example 13f:

Here's a much trickier lick on the D chord in the next section. The lick begins with the slide, but then plays three notes fretted with the fingers before playing the open strings and sliding up to the 12th fret. It will take time to get that to feel natural, but it's a perfect example of what can be achieved using the slide and fingers together.

Example 13g:

After two passes through the whole form, I've ended the performance with a final run through the first eight bars, with a slight variation on the melody. Gradually slow the piece down as you come to an end for a feeling of completion. Listen to the audio to hear how this should sound.

Example 13h:

Progressing from here is just a case of listening, copying and experimenting.

Listen to as many recordings and videos as you can find of people playing this song form (however, not the Merle Travis *Cannonball Rag* which often comes up when searching!)

The more comfortable you are with the style, the more fluent you'll become adding your own licks and phrases to the music. Take every opportunity to put your own stamp on the tune, express yourself and play the music that you want to hear.

Good luck!

Conclusion

You should now be well on your way to having a solid understanding of the wild world of Delta blues slide playing.

However, as with any book like this, you're not at the end of the journey. In fact, you've just begun and there's still a long path to walk before you'll feel right at home in this genre. The fascinating thing about this style of playing is just how hard it is to imitate authentically. The people who played this music really didn't know much about music theory, so it's a style that is learnt more by *listening* and *doing*.

You only need to listen to a few Son House or Bukka White recordings to hear that this is a genre that can be simple and complex at the same time. Usually this comes to individual style. Each player had their own approach to hitting the strings. Some Delta bluesmen were precise fingerstyle players, while others were wild and percussive. Son House was so aggressive he would treat his guitar like a drum. Bukka White would flail his arm from bridge to nut when strumming. There's something to be said for the dynamic rage these legends were capable of, even if they were less concerned with things like structure and harmony!

The twelve-bar form was far from established at this period in time. The chords tended to follow the vocal wherever it led. It's not uncommon to hear someone sit on the I chord for ten bars, then go to the IV chord for three bars, then back to the I. The key is listening. Listen, listen, then listen some more. The most effective way to learn to speak a language is to hear it in context.

You have to hear this music to really understand it, otherwise you'll stand out like a sore thumb among the purists. Thankfully, most of this music is from the '20s and '30s and is easy to find online on sites like YouTube or Spotify. You'll pick up CDs for pennies and the charity shops are full of them. There's no excuse for hiding from it, even if it's just a cheap compilation CD (a rarity in 2018!)

To get you started, here are some recommendations of artists and albums to listen to. Most of the names here all predate the traditional album format, so many will be compilations of singles they released in their time. Don't be worried, it's all above board!

- Sylvester Weaver – Complete Recorded Works in Chronological Order Volume 1

- Robert Johnson – The Complete Recordings

- Son House – Son House Library of Congress Recordings 1941 – 1942

- Bukka White – High Fever Blues: The Complete 1930 – 1940 Recordings

- Blind Willie Johnson – The Spiritual Blues

- Blind Willie McTell – King Of The Serpent Blues

- Tampa Red – You Can't Get That Stuff No More

- Charley Patton – The Definitive Charley Patton

- Blind Boy Fuller – Get Your Yas Yas Out

- Leadbelly – The Very Best of Leadbelly

- Elmore James – The Sky Is Crying

- Muddy Waters – The Chess Singles Collection

- Lightnin' Hopkins – Dirty House Blues

When you've got the sound deep in your soul, it's all about experimentation. There's rarely anything so complicated that it can't be worked out with a little exploration. The longer you play, the more of a connection you'll develop between your fingers and your ears, and then you'll really be cooking!

If all else fails, you can always head on down to the crossroads and make a deal…

Good luck!

Levi

Other Books by Levi Clay

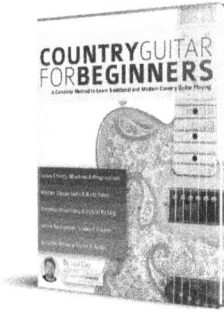

Country Guitar for Beginners is a complete guide to help beginners master elements of the country genre. Split into two sections, this book is designed to develop chord playing, rhythm guitar skills and lead guitar solos.

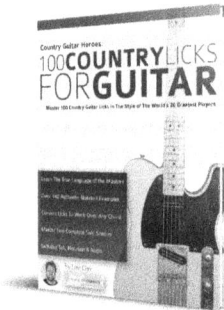

100 Country Licks for Guitar goes way beyond most normal 'boring' lick books… you will learn authentic country guitar licks "In the style of" the 20 greatest country guitarists…ever. What's more, you'll learn how to form their licks into your own personal language… in any key and in any style.

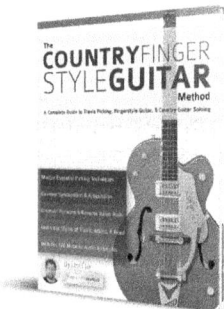

The Country Fingerstyle Guitar Method is the perfect way to master finger picking on the guitar. Part One tackles the techniques and skills needed to build confidence, speed and articulation when playing Country Guitar. Part Two takes a detailed look at the evolution of Country Guitar Fingerstyle and studies the styles and idiosyncrasies of artists Merle Travis, Chet Atkins and Jerry Reed. Each artist's approach to Country Guitar is dissected and through multiple 'in the style of' examples.

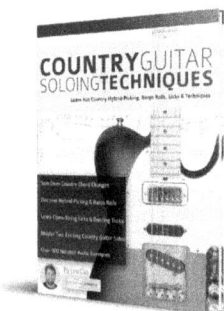

Country Guitar Soloing Techniques takes you on a journey of discovery that teaches you authentic country guitar soloing using the actual techniques of the masters. With over 100 notated audio examples, every essential technique, scale and approach is dissected and developed into musical licks and exciting, flamboyant solos.

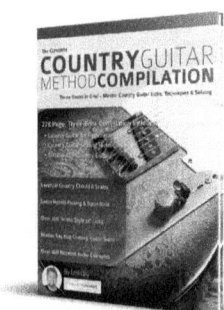

The Complete Country Guitar Method Compilation is a collection of three best-selling books that teach the essential skills, techniques and theory required to move from absolute basics to astonishing country guitar solos. With 278 jam-packed pages and 400 notated audio examples, this is the most comprehensible guide to country guitar playing ever.